EUREKA!
I've discovered
FORCE

Todd Plummer

mc **Marshall Cavendish**
Benchmark

New York

Marshall Cavendish Benchmark
99 White Plains Road
Tarrytown, NY 10591
www.marshallcavendish.us

All Internet addresses were available and accurate when this book went to press.

Library of Congress Cataloging-in-Publication Data
Plummer, Todd.
I've discovered force! / by Todd Plummer.
p. cm. -- (Eureka!)
Includes bibliographical references and index.
ISBN 978-0-7614-3204-3
1. Force and energy--Juvenile literature. I. Title.
QC73.4.P58 2009
531'.6--dc22
2008014540

Cover: Q2A Media Art Bank and Marilyn Volan/Shutterstock
Half Title : Q2A Media Art Bank
NASA/Science Photo Library: P7; Wouter van Caspel/istockphoto: P7tr;
Serge Brunier (TWAN)/NASA: P11; Shepard Mitchell/NASA/Ap images: P11br;
Mary Evans Picture Library/Alamy: P12; Science Photo Library/Photolibrary: P15tr;
prism_68/Shutterstock: P15;
Jeff McDonald/Istockphoto: P19; James Steidl/Shutterstock: P20; Roman Krochuk/
Shutterstock: P23; Glenda M. Powers/Shutterstock: P27
Illustrations: Q2A Media Art Bank

Created by Q2AMedia
Creative Director: Simmi Sikka
Series Editor: Jessica Cohn
Art Director: Sudakshina Basu
Designer: Dibakar Acharjee
Illustrators: Amit Tayal, Aadil Ahmed, Rishi Bhardwaj,
Kusum Kala, Pooja Shukla and Sanyogita Lal
Photo research: Sejal Sehgal
Senior Project Manager: Ravneet Kaur
Project Manager: Shekhar Kapur

Printed in Malaysia

1 3 5 6 4 2

Contents

The Nature of Force

Look around and what do you see? Cars and airplanes zip around. Leaves blow in the wind. Buildings seem to stand still. **Forces** are acting on all of these things, all the time. They even act on the building.

A force is anything that makes a push or a pull. You can't see forces; you see their effects. If two equally strong forces act on something, but in opposite directions, they stop each other. For example, when you clap your hands, the force of one hand stops the other hand's force.

We give forces many different names. **Friction** is the opposite motion between two surfaces in contact. In other words, two things rub. Some other familiar forces include **gravity, electricity, magnetism, mechanical force,** and air pressure.

People have been thinking about forces for ages. Aristotle was a famous thinker in ancient Greece. He spent a lot of time thinking about the natural forces of the world.

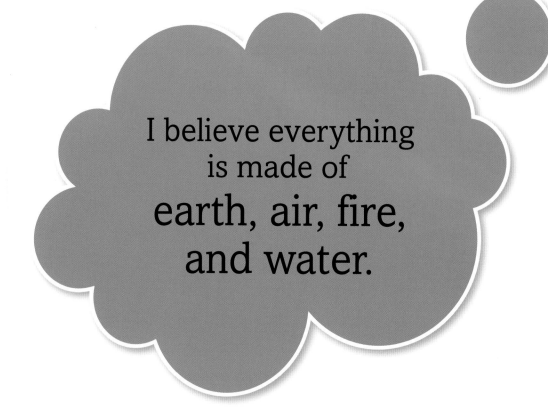

I believe everything is made of **earth, air, fire, and water.**

Meet Aristotle

Aristotle's (384–322 b.c.e.) ideas influenced the understanding of nature and math for more than two thousand years. His theory of **metaphysics** was that everything was made up of earth, air, fire, and water. He knew nothing of **atoms** or chemical **elements**. He just believed, based on what he saw around him, that natural forces resulted from earth, air, fire, and water finding their place in the world. Water flows down. Air rises through water. Dirt sinks in water. Aristotle rarely did experiments, and many of his ideas were proven wrong. Yet he got people thinking.

Tug of War and Friction

You Will Need:

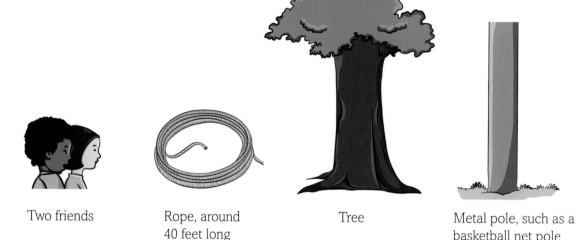

Two friends

Rope, around 40 feet long

Tree

Metal pole, such as a basketball net pole

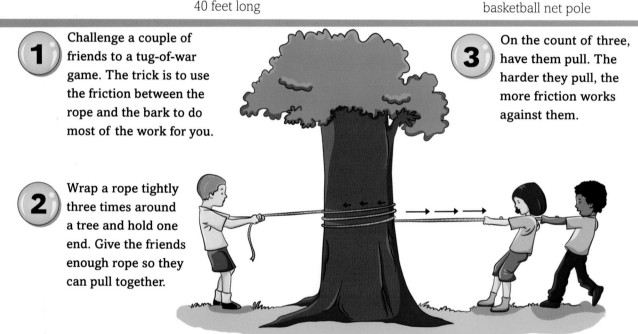

1 Challenge a couple of friends to a tug-of-war game. The trick is to use the friction between the rope and the bark to do most of the work for you.

2 Wrap a rope tightly three times around a tree and hold one end. Give the friends enough rope so they can pull together.

3 On the count of three, have them pull. The harder they pull, the more friction works against them.

4 Next, try this experiment with a smooth metal pole instead of a tree. The friction will be much less.

WHO WOULD HAVE THOUGHT?

Friction is often thought of as wasted energy. Yet many useful devices are based on friction. Sandpaper makes good use of friction. People use sandpaper to grind down surfaces, such as wood that needs a new stain. Striking a match is using friction to make a flame. Without friction, you would not last long. Friction makes it possible for you to walk. Without it, everything you touch would be slicker than ice. You couldn't hold a fork or a pencil. Your socks would fall off. Rockets and just about everything else would have to be built differently.

What's the Matter?

Forces act on **matter**, which is anything that has **mass** and takes up space. Mass is a measure of how many and what kinds of atoms something is made of. You are familiar with three states of matter: solids, liquids, and gases. Each reacts differently to forces. Squeeze a block of wood (solid), a half-filled plastic bottle of water (liquid), and a blown-up balloon (gas). The wood keeps its shape and size. The **pressure** you apply changes the shape of the bottle. The water keeps its mass but takes a new shape within the bottle. The air in the balloon spreads out or presses together to fill its container.

Sometimes the best thoughts about force have come to people at odd moments. If you could talk to Archimedes, one of the greatest scientists of the ancient world, he would tell you . . .

Meet Archimedes

Archimedes' (287–212 B.C.E.) inventions include the crane and a pulley system called the block and tackle. He made a very clever device used for lifting water, too. Archimedes also observed how different objects floated—or didn't! He found that the **buoyancy** of an object is determined by its shape and weight. An object in water pushes aside, or displaces, a certain amount of water. It is buoyed up or pushed up by a force equal to the weight of the water it displaces. If the object is heavier than that amount of water, it will sink. If it is lighter, it will float. We call this **Archimedes' principle.**

King Hieron had asked me to figure out if his new crown was really solid gold.

While thinking about how I would do that, I took my bath.

I noticed that when I sank into the tub, the water rose and overflowed.

Eureka
is Greek for
"I have found it!"

Now, this may not amaze you, but it was a eureka moment for me.

I ran to test the crown in water to see how much water it would displace.

I got an equal weight of pure gold and tested that.
The crown displaced more water.
It was not the same kind of metal!

Buoyancy

You Will Need:

2 squares of aluminum foil, about 8 inches per side

Sink or large bowl filled with water

 1 Roll one sheet of foil into a tight ball. Drop it into the water. What does it do?

2 Mold the second sheet into a "boat." Does it float? If not, reshape it.

3 A boat is wide, compared to a ball. A boat floats.

4 Consider: The two pieces of foil weighed the same. But the foil ball is smaller than the boat. Both items displaced water. But the water the boat displaced weighed more than the foil of the boat. So the boat floated.

WHO WOULD HAVE THOUGHT?

For an extreme example of the way forces act on matter, look to space. Far beyond Earth, scientists have found **black holes**. These discoveries are not really holes. They are objects with so much **gravity,** or pull, that even light cannot escape from them. These objects have more mass than a billion suns. The more mass something has, the stronger its gravity. So the pull of these objects is strong! Some black holes come from stars that have burned out and fallen inward. Even bigger black holes form in the centers of galaxies. Scientists are not yet sure about the state of matter in a black hole.

Forces All Around Us

Machines make work easier. They typically consist of one or more **simple machines:** wheel and axle, **lever,** wedge, inclined plane (ramp), pulley, or screw. Galileo used ramps to study how things act while in motion. Ramps don't have moving parts, but they help with movement. It is easier to pull or push a load up a ramp than it is to carry the load up steps. When Galileo died, Sir Isaac Newton was born. He used Galileo's work to help write three laws of motion:

1. *An object at rest tends to stay at rest, and an object that is moving will keep on moving in a straight line unless some force acts on it.* **If you skip a rock across a frozen pond, the rock slides until it hits something or is stopped by friction.**

2. *A force will cause an object to **accelerate**, or speed up. The bigger the force, the greater the acceleration. The same force will accelerate lighter objects faster than heavier objects.* **This makes sense. The harder you hit a tennis ball, the faster the ball shoots off. If you whack a cannonball, it barely moves.**

3. *Every force has an equal and opposite reaction force.* **When you place a book on a table, gravity pulls the book downward. Yet the table pushes upward. So the book stays on the table. Forces tend to come in pairs**.

I worked with pendulums, too.

Meet Galileo Galilei

Aristotle thought heavy objects fell faster than lighter ones. Galileo (1564–1642), an Italian thinker, proved Aristotle wrong. Legend says Galileo experimented by dropping items off the Leaning Tower of Pisa. Yet it is more likely he rolled balls of various weights down long ramps and timed them. All objects, he said, speed up as they fall, due to gravity. They all speed up at the same rate, too. Galileo also built a telescope to study space. His observations of Jupiter's moons told him that the Sun, not Earth, was the center of the solar system.

ROUND AND ROUND IT GOES!

Experiment with a Lever

You Will Need:

Yardstick, meterstick, or long wooden handle

Rubber band

Pair of shoes with shoelaces

1 Tie the shoes together by the shoestrings. With one finger under the tie, lift the shoes a few inches to feel how much force is needed to lift them.

2 Next, wrap the rubber band around the yardstick about six inches from one end, to keep the shoes from sliding.

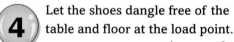

3 Place that end of the stick on the edge of a counter or table. The point where it rests will be the **fulcrum**. That will be the point of rotation. You will drape the shoes on the stick just above the rubber band (load point).

4 Let the shoes dangle free of the table and floor at the load point.

5 With one finger, lift the other end of the yardstick (lift point) about 2 feet.

6 It was easier—right? Try moving the shoes closer to the lifting end. Notice what happens.

WHO WOULD HAVE THOUGHT?

Early clocks ran with gears, or wheels with teeth. Gears are simple machines, too. If you put two gears together, with the teeth locked in place, one can turn the other. Galileo invented a new kind of clock, too, but his was not mechanical. In 1610, he discovered four tiny "stars" circling Jupiter. Over several weeks, he discovered that each was a moon, moving in an **orbit**. The orbits lasted the same time each time. He figured out how to use these moons as a clock to tell what time it was. His "clock" helped explorers navigate for hundreds of years.

Feeling Down

"Down" is down because of gravity. That is a force related to the mass and size of Earth. Isaac Newton discovered that everything in the universe pulls on everything else. The more mass a space body like Earth has, the more gravity, or pull, it has. Nearby things pull more than do distant things, so Earth pulls on us.

The force of gravity on anything with mass is measured as weight. Weight changes depending on the mass of whatever is doing the pulling. More mass means more weight. Objects on the moon weigh one-sixth of what they weigh on Earth.

Gravity holds together stars, solar systems, even galaxies. Without gravity, these things would fly apart. Anything not glued down would float away. If Newton were alive and could explain it all . . .

Meet Isaac Newton

Many people consider the Englishman Isaac Newton (about 1643–1727) to be the greatest scientist ever. Besides the laws of motion and his discoveries about gravity, he helped invent an advanced system of math called **calculus.** He discovered the nature of color and invented the reflecting telescope. Later in life, he spent years trying to turn metals like lead into gold, which we now know is impossible. Even geniuses make mistakes!

WHY ME?

I was wondering how the moon stayed in orbit around Earth. What hidden forces were at work?

Then came that fateful day. I saw an apple fall from a tree.

I already knew about gravity.

Suddenly it made sense: The same force that pulled the apple also kept the moon going around Earth. The moon was really falling, but Earth was pulling it along.

Gravity kept the planets orbiting the Sun.

What a Drag!

You Will Need:

Notebook paper

Hardcover book that is the same size as the paper or larger

Cotton balls, feathers, similar light objects

Pencil or pen

1 Hold a piece of paper in one hand. Hold a book in the other. The flat side of each item must be parallel to the floor. Drop both from the same height. **Drag** is a force that works against these moving objects. Which hits the floor first?

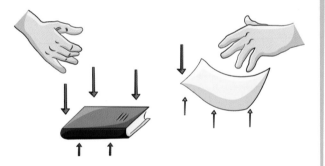

2 Consider: The upward force of drag relates to the area of the falling object. It relates to the mass, too. The book and the paper have the same area. Yet the paper has less mass, so it is affected more.

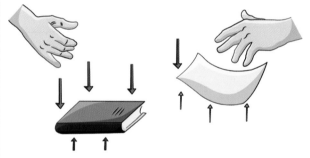

3 Next, place a piece of notebook paper flat on the book. Drop them together. What happens? The notebook deflects the drag, and the paper falls with it.

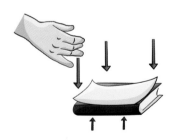

4 Try it with light objects such as cotton balls and feathers on top of the notebook. Make notes about what happens in each case. Then think about the differences.

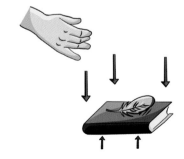

WHO WOULD HAVE THOUGHT?

In a **vacuum,** where there is no air, all objects fall at the same rate. In the atmosphere, air plays a role in the speed of the fall. Falling objects speed up at first. Then they reach a point when the force of gravity is opposed by drag. Skydivers know all about drag, because they fall through air, too. Joseph Kittinger was a U.S. Air Force pilot in the early 1960s. He holds the world record for fastest free fall. He jumped out of a hot air balloon at 102,800 feet (31,333 meters). That's at the edge of outer space. He reached speeds of 614 miles (988 kilometers) per hour before he opened his parachute.

Charge It!

The center of an atom is made of **protons**, with a positive charge, and (usually) **neutrons**, which have no charge. **Electrons** are tiny particles with negative charges. They surround protons and neutrons like flies. Opposite charges attract each other, so protons (+) are attracted to electrons (−). Similar charges push each other apart.

When an atom has the same number of protons and electrons, it is balanced. The atom is held together by its electric force. The electrons of some materials can detach from the atom and move freely. That can happen with most metals. The electrons flow through the material.

Electricity is a form of energy that involves the flow of electrons. The flowing electrons transmit electrical energy from one point to another. To control electricity, we use a generator or a battery to keep the electrons moving.

The flip side of electricity is magnetism. Magnets are objects that have at least two poles (+/−) and a magnetic field. That is an area where magnetism is detected. Earth is a huge magnet. It has a North Pole (+) and a South Pole (−).

Magnets come in all sizes, from the little magnets used to hold papers on a refrigerator to Earth. Magnets have all kinds of uses, too. They can even move trains over a magnetized track. Maglev (**mag**netic **lev**itation) trains are the fastest trains in the world, reaching speeds of over 350 miles (563 kilometers) per hour.

Old ideas about magnets were wrong.

Meet the Magnetic Personalities

Each of these men made important discoveries in the field of electricity and magnetism.

William Gilbert (1544–1603), an English doctor shown below, wrote *On the Magnet*, the first great book on electricity and magnetism. He discovered that compasses work because Earth is a giant magnet. Until Gilbert, it was thought that garlic stopped magnets!

Benjamin Franklin (1706–1790) was an American statesman and scientist. He proved lightning is electricity when he famously (and foolishly) flew a kite in a thunderstorm. He figured out that electricity has positive and negative charges.

Alessandro Volta (1745–1827) was an Italian pioneer in electrical engineering. He studied the relationship between chemistry and electricity. He invented the first battery. The **volt**, which measures electrical charge, is named after him.

Michael Faraday (1791–1867) was an English scientist. He discovered that moving magnets could create electricity. He showed that electricity can create magnetism in a piece of metal. He invented the first basic electrical motor.

James Clerk Maxwell (1831–1879) was Scottish. He wrote four mathematical rules of electricity and magnetism, based on past discoveries. He also discovered that light is a form of electromagnetic energy.

Homemade Compass

You Will Need:

Sewing needle   Magnet   Cooking oil   Bottle cork in case oil doesn't work   Bucket of water

1 Drag a thin needle in one direction about thirty times across the magnet. This will turn the needle into a magnet for a very short time.

2 Coat the needle with a drop of oil. Carefully put the needle on the surface of the water.

3 If this doesn't work, tape it to the cork and float it. It will slowly rotate until it points north and south.

4 Bring the magnet close to the needle and watch what happens. This is why magnets need to be kept away from compasses. Keep magnets away from computer screens, credit cards, and video and audio tapes, too.

WHO WOULD HAVE THOUGHT?

Earth's core is liquid metal. The flow of molten metal in the core makes a magnetic field around Earth. That huge magnetic field has invisible lines of force. The lines flow between the North Pole and the South Pole. These poles do not stay in the same places. Right now, the North Pole is moving from northern Canada toward Siberia. The magnetic field grows stronger and weaker, too. Yet the field redirects many harmful rays from the Sun away from the planet. Some of those rays mix with the magnetic field miles above Earth. That makes the light show known as the northern lights, shown here.

Water and Air

Turn on the water and stick your finger in the end of a hose. The water shoots out faster and farther. By shrinking the opening, you increase pressure, the force applied over an area. Water pressure increases with depth in the ocean, too. In the deepest ocean, the pressure is more than a thousand times what it is at the surface—enough to crush steel.

The atmosphere, like an ocean of air, pushes in all directions. If you are in a plane, the air pressure is less. Higher pressure air behind your ear-drums tries to get into lower pressure air outside. Liquids and gases such as air flow from areas of higher pressure to areas of lower pressure.

The same forces work to keep airplanes in the air. Wings are curved on top and flat on the bottom. So air on top moves faster over a greater distance than air below. Daniel Bernoulli (1700–1782), a Swiss scientist shown on page 25, discovered that the faster a fluid moves, the lower its pressure. Air is a fluid. Beneath an airplane's wing, air moves more slowly. So there is greater pressure below the wings than above. The result is a force called lift that pushes the wings upward.

When air moves over the surface of a bird's wing as the bird glides, the air goes faster over the top than it does below.

Meet Otto von Guericke

Otto von Guericke (1602–1686), a German scientist, is famous for discovering a way to make . . . nothing. Sometime around 1650, he invented the first vacuum pump. It sucked all the molecules from a tightly closed container so that absolutely nothing was left behind. He developed the modern **barometer**, too, which measures air pressure. Aristotle, long before, had said "nature abhors a vacuum." He meant that he thought space must always be occupied by *something*. Yet he was wrong about that. Guericke proved it.

Light as Air Pressure

You Will Need:

Saucer or other
lid for glass

Glass

Water

---

1 Try this over a sink! Fill a glass to the brim, until it is almost overflowing. Cover it with a saucer or a plastic lid. A little water may get out, but make sure there is no air in the glass.

2 Now, hold the lid tight with one hand and carefully turn the glass over. Let go of the lid. The lid stays on the glass all by itself.

3 Consider: Water is pressing down. Air pressure is pushing up on the lid. The water and lid together push down with their combined weight of a few ounces.

4 The air wins, until a little air gets under the lid. Now, try to jiggle the lid or saucer a bit. What happens? (You were warned!)

WHO WOULD HAVE THOUGHT?

When you drink through a straw, you make a vacuum. You don't actually pull the drink into your mouth. It is pushed up the straw by the air pressing down on the liquid in your cup. A similar force is at work in the atmosphere. Atmospheric pressure helps us breathe. It pushes on our chests so our lungs press inward. The carbon dioxide is forced out. During a tornado, fast spinning air creates low pressure. It is so low that it can cause people to black out. It sucks the air right out of their lungs. The forces of nature are amazing.

Timeline

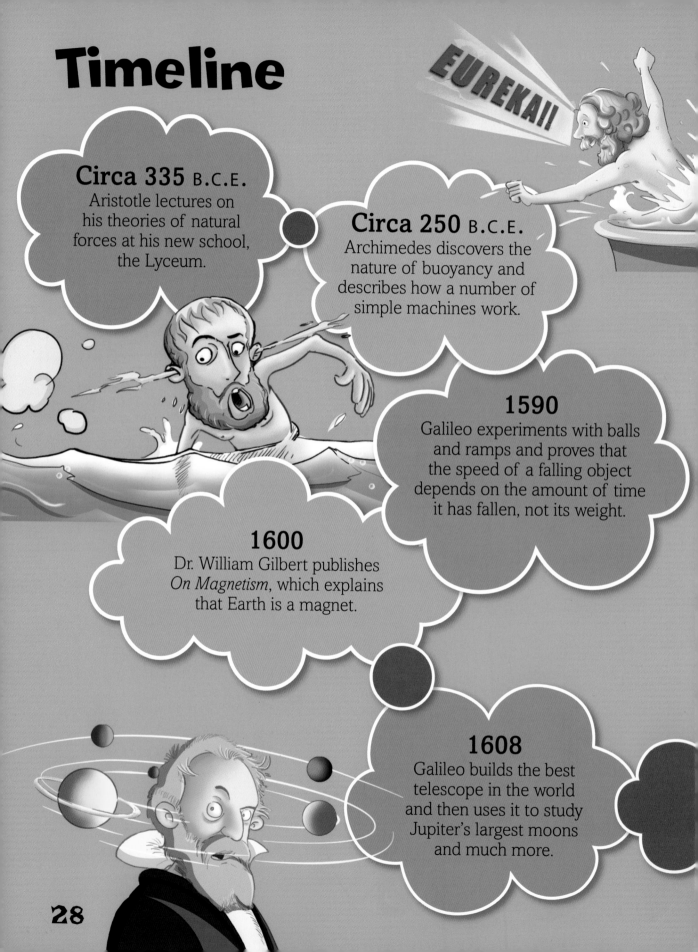

EUREKA!!

Circa 335 B.C.E.
Aristotle lectures on his theories of natural forces at his new school, the Lyceum.

Circa 250 B.C.E.
Archimedes discovers the nature of buoyancy and describes how a number of simple machines work.

1590
Galileo experiments with balls and ramps and proves that the speed of a falling object depends on the amount of time it has fallen, not its weight.

1600
Dr. William Gilbert publishes *On Magnetism*, which explains that Earth is a magnet.

1608
Galileo builds the best telescope in the world and then uses it to study Jupiter's largest moons and much more.

1905
Albert Einstein shows that Newton's laws of motion break down as objects approach the speed of light.

1861
James Clerk Maxwell publishes his famous equations on electricity and magnetism in a paper titled *On Physical Lines of Force.*

1821
Michael Faraday presents the first-ever electrical motor.

1800
Alessandro Volta invents the first wet-cell battery.

1750
Ben Franklin proposes that lightning is a form of electricity and later proves it experimentally.

1687
Isaac Newton publishes *The Principia,* which explains gravity and the laws of motion in great detail.

1650
Otto von Guericke builds the first vacuum pump.

Glossary

accelerate To speed up.

Archimedes' principle An object in a fluid is buoyed up by a force equal to the weight of the fluid displaced by the object.

atom Smallest particle of an element that has all the characteristics of that element.

barometer Device that measures air pressure to predict possible weather changes.

black hole Space object with so much gravitational pull, not even light can escape.

buoyancy Tendency of an object to rise or float in a fluid.

calculus Type of advanced math that especially deals with rates of change.

drag Force that acts against a body in motion, slowing it down.

electricity Force brought about by the movement of electrons.

electron Particle in an atom that has a negative charge.

element Basic substance that consists of atoms of only one kind.

force Push or pull that tends to change the speed or direction of motion of something.

friction Force that resists motion between two surfaces rubbing against each other.

fulcrum Point of support or rotation on a lever.

gravity The attraction of the mass of a heavenly body for other bodies near its surface.

lever Simple machine used to lift or pry; operated by applying effort on one point as the lever rotates on its fulcrum.

magnetism Power to attract certain metals or produce a magnetic field, created by a magnet or a conductor with an electric current.

mass Amount of matter in an object.

matter Anything that takes up space and has mass.

mechanical force Force resulting from machines.

metaphysics Philosophy concerned with the basic nature of things.

neutron Particle in atom that has no charge.

orbit To circle around something.

pressure Amount of force applied over an area or against an opposing force.

proton Particle in atom that has a positive charge.

simple machine Basic device that needs only a single force to work; used in combination to construct all other machines.

vacuum Space that is completely empty of any kind of matter.

volt Unit of measure in electricity.

Index